EASY
ENGLISH
VOCABULARY
GAMES

Linda Schinke-Llano

Printed on recyclable paper

PASSPORT BOOKS
a division of *NTC Publishing Group*
Lincolnwood, Illinois USA

1997 Printing

Published by Passport Books, a division of NTC Publishing Group.
© 1992 by NTC Publishing Group, 4255 West Touhy Avenue,
Lincolnwood (Chicago), Illinois 60646-1975 U.S.A.
Manufactured in the United States of America.

7 8 9 0 VP 9 8 7 6 5

INTRODUCTION

Easy English Vocabulary Games is filled with 70 fun games and puzzles to help you practice and review your English-language skills.

Many of the games focus on the vocabulary you need to talk about special interests and hobbies such as music, movies, and sports. Other games review the essential vocabulary you need for a wide range of everyday activities such as following directions, reading newspaper ads, and shopping. In addition, some of the games help you practice important language structures and verb tenses.

Each game has clear, easy-to-follow directions and an example to help you get started. And, if you would like to check your answers, you will find a complete Answer Key at the back of the book.

CONTENTS

WHO AM I?

DIRECTIONS: Answer the questions. Use the pictures to help you.

Example: I bake cakes. Who am I?   _____baker_____

1. I teach school. Who am I?   _____
2. I cut hair. Who am I?   _____
3. I put out fires. Who am I?   _____
4. I pick up garbage. Who am I?   _____
5. I bring your mail. Who am I?   _____
6. I direct traffic. Who am I?   _____
7. I fix teeth. Who am I?   _____
8. I help sick people. Who am I?   _____
9. I grow your food. Who am I?   _____
10. I cook food. Who am I?   _____

2

RIDDLES

DIRECTIONS: Change the first letter. Make a new word.

Example: RED: Change the first letter.
                          Make something we sleep in.   ____bed____

1. FAN   Change the first letter.
            Make something we cook in.   _____

2. FISH   Change the first letter.
            Make something we eat on.   _____

3. RUB   Change the first letter.
            Make something we take a bath in.   _____

4. FAR   Change the first letter.
            Make something we ride in.   _____

5. TEN   Change the first letter.
            Make something we write with.   _____

6. BOY   Change the first letter.
            Make something we play with.   _____

7. TOP   Change the first letter.
            Make something we clean the floor with.   _____

8. DAMP   Change the first letter.
            Make something that gives light.   _____

9. LOOK   Change the first letter.
            Make something that we read.   _____

10. FAT   Change the first letter.
            Make something that says "mee-ow."   _____

11. FOG   Change the first letter.
            Make something that barks.   _____

12. MOUSE   Change the first letter.
            Make something we live in.   _____

13. BOAT   Change the first letter.
            Make something we wear.   _____

14. COOL   Change the first letter.
            Make something we swim in.   _____

15. SILK   Change the first letter.
            Make something we drink.   _____

PREPOSITIONS

DIRECTIONS: Circle the right answer.

Example: The cat is ____in____ the box.

on
(in)
under

1. The glove is _____ the table.
   on
   in
   under

2. The table is _____ the chair.
   behind
   in front of
   beside

3. The dog is _____ the chair.
   under
   above
   in

4. The hat is _____ the bed.
   beside
   on top of
   in

5. The flowers are _____ the house.
   behind
   above
   in front of

6. The fish is _____ the lake.
   in
   on
   below

7. The plane is _____ the clouds.
   next to
   above
   below

8. The ribbon is _____ the package.
   in
   next to
   around

9. The saucer is _____ the cup.
   beneath
   above
   in front of

4

LET'S COMPARE

DIRECTIONS: Fill in the blank with the correct word.

Example: _____John_____ is shorter than _____Dick_____ .

1. _____ 's hair is longer than _____ 's hair.

2. _____ is younger than _____ .

3. _____ is wider than _____ .

4. _____ is thinner than _____ .

5. _____ is stronger than _____ .

6. _____ is newer than _____ .

7. _____ is the heaviest box.

8. _____ is the smallest ball.

9. _____ is the tallest building.

10. _____ is the biggest book.

John

Dick

Rita

Carol

George

Tom

House A

House B

Sparky

Jocko

Jim

Bob

Mary's car

Ken's car

A 50 lbs.   B 2000 lbs.   C 500 lbs.

A   B   C

A   B   C

A   B   C

THE TELEPHONE

DIRECTIONS: Use the chart to find the names of the parts of the telephone. A side number and a top number together show you the letter. (For example, 14=D.) Then find the part on the drawing at the bottom.

	1	2	3	4	5
1	A	B	C	D	E
2	F	G	H	I	J
3	K	L	M	N	O
4	P	Q	R	S	T
5	U	V	W	X	Y/Z

1. 14 24 11 32

2. 43 15 13 15 24 52 15 43

3. 13 35 43 14

4. 13 35 24 34   44 32 35 45

5. 13 35 24 34   43 15 45 51 43 34

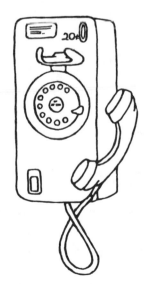

1. ___dial_____

2. _____

3. _____

4. _____

5. _____

6

VERB FIT-IN

DIRECTIONS: Put the correct verb in the boxes on the right.

Example: I _____ my homework last night.
(do)

1. I _____ my books from first grade.
(keep)

2. The telephone _____ a lot last night.
(ring)

3. The boy _____ his gloves yesterday.
(lose)

4. We _____ for three hours in church last Sunday.
(sit)

5. I _____ her last year.
(meet)

6. She _____ me a package last week.
(send)

7. The Warriors _____ the basketball game.
(win)

8. They _____ their house for a lot of money.
(sell)

9. He _____ his new sweater yesterday.
(wear)

10. George _____ fast last night.
(drive)

11. We _____ breakfast late this morning.
(eat)

12. I _____ her name yesterday afternoon.
(forget)

13. Susan _____ a new car last year.
(buy)

14. He _____ one hundred miles last summer.
(swim)

D I D

OPPOSITES

DIRECTIONS: Below are incomplete words. Add letters from the bottom. Make words that are opposites.
(Note: Some letters are used more than one time.)

Example: __b__ lack   __w__ hite

1. ___ in   ___ ose   9. ___ ry   ___ et

2. ___ ive   ___ ake   10. ___ bove   ___ elow

3. ___ uy   ___ ell   11. ___ ark   ___ ight

4. ___ ork   ___ lay   12. ___ old   ___ ot

5. ___ it   ___ tand   13. ___ retty   ___ gly

6. ___ sk   ___ nswer   14. ___ ew   ___ ld

7. ___ ight   ___ eft   15. ___ oft   ___ ard

8. ___ sleep   ___ wake

a b c d g h l n o p r s t u w

TIME

DIRECTIONS: Answer the following questions. Use the clocks to help you.

Example: How long did the baby sleep?

          three hours

midnight   am

1 How long did George study?

pm   pm

2. How long did Grace practice the piano?

pm   pm

3. How many hours did the class last?

am   am

4. How many hours was the TV program on?

noon   pm

5. How many minutes did the cake bake?

pm   pm

6. How many minutes does Ellen have for lunch?

pm   pm

7. How long does Joe work every day?

am   pm

8. How long do they spend in school every day?

am   pm

BUILD A WORD

DIRECTIONS: Make new words. Add the letter(s) to the word for the picture.

Example: w +   _____hat_____ = _____what_____

1. p +   _____ = _____

2. h +   _____ = _____

3. st +   _____ = _____

4. s +   _____ = _____

5. s +   _____ = _____

6. d +   _____ = _____

7. s +   _____ = _____

8. f +   _____ = _____

9. d +   _____ = _____

10. t +   _____ = _____

RELATIONSHIPS

DIRECTIONS: Use the letters in the boxes to complete the words. Cross out the letters that you use. The letters left will spell a word. Write that word at the bottom.

~~p~~	re	su	em	la	pa
ch	ti	cu	on	st	au
te	sh	pl	ip	s	░░

driver   _p_ assenger

teacher   ___ udent

doctor   ___ tient

clerk   ___ stomer

coach   ___ ayer

king   ___ bject

actor   ___ dience

landlord   ___ nant

parent   ___ ild

employer   ___ ployee

— — — — — — — — — — — — —

WHERE ARE YOU?

DIRECTIONS: Follow the directions. Use the map below.

Go to the start.

Drive north.

Turn west on Maple Street.

Go two blocks.

Turn right.

Drive three blocks.

Turn east.

Where are you? _____

WORD STAIRS

DIRECTIONS: Use the words at the bottom to make stairsteps. How many can you make?

Example: T O P
                   I
            N O W

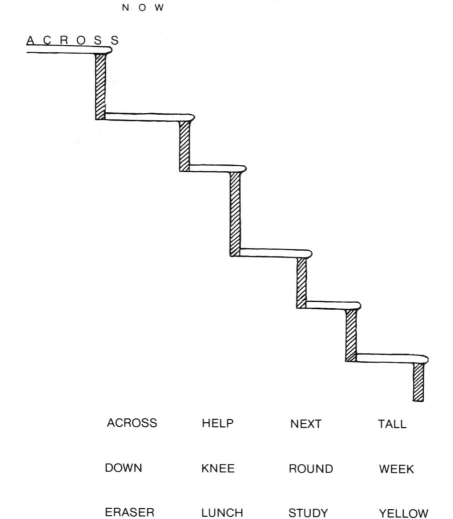

A C R O S S

ACROSS	HELP	NEXT	TALL
DOWN	KNEE	ROUND	WEEK
ERASER	LUNCH	STUDY	YELLOW

ANIMALS

DIRECTIONS: Unscramble the letters to make the name of an animal. The pictures will help you.

Example: A   C   T   ___cat___

1. N   A   T   _____

2. G   O   R   F   _____

3. P   A   T   H   E   L   E   N   _____

4. S   O   R   E   H   _____

5. B   A   R   I   B   T   _____

6. B   A   R   E   Z   _____

7. L   O   W   _____

8. R   E   E   D   _____

9. W   O   C   _____

10. D   R   I   B   _____

11. N   E   C   K   I   C   H   _____

12. F   L   U   T   Y   B   E   R   T   _____

14

2 + 2

DIRECTIONS: Draw a line from the words at the left to the correct symbol at the right.

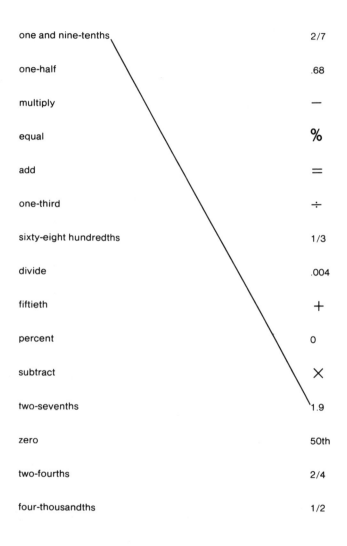

one and nine-tenths	2/7
one-half	.68
multiply	—
equal	%
add	=
one-third	÷
sixty-eight hundredths	1/3
divide	.004
fiftieth	+
percent	0
subtract	X
two-sevenths	1.9
zero	50th
two-fourths	2/4
four-thousandths	1/2

MONEY

DIRECTIONS: Write the names of the coins and bills in the blanks. Then write the correct letters in the numbered blanks at the bottom of the page.

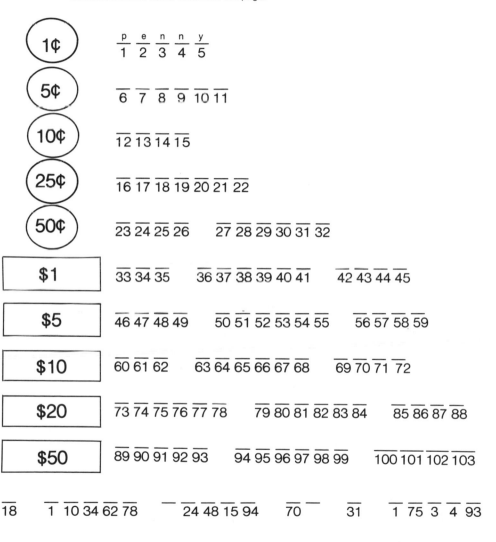

1¢

$$\frac{p}{1}\ \frac{e}{2}\ \frac{n}{3}\ \frac{n}{4}\ \frac{y}{5}$$

5¢

$$\overline{6}\ \overline{7}\ \overline{8}\ \overline{9}\ \overline{10}\ \overline{11}$$

10¢

$$\overline{12}\ \overline{13}\ \overline{14}\ \overline{15}$$

25¢

$$\overline{16}\ \overline{17}\ \overline{18}\ \overline{19}\ \overline{20}\ \overline{21}\ \overline{22}$$

50¢

$$\overline{23}\ \overline{24}\ \overline{25}\ \overline{26}\qquad \overline{27}\ \overline{28}\ \overline{29}\ \overline{30}\ \overline{31}\ \overline{32}$$

$1

$$\overline{33}\ \overline{34}\ \overline{35}\qquad \overline{36}\ \overline{37}\ \overline{38}\ \overline{39}\ \overline{40}\ \overline{41}\qquad \overline{42}\ \overline{43}\ \overline{44}\ \overline{45}$$

$5

$$\overline{46}\ \overline{47}\ \overline{48}\ \overline{49}\qquad \overline{50}\ \overline{51}\ \overline{52}\ \overline{53}\ \overline{54}\ \overline{55}\qquad \overline{56}\ \overline{57}\ \overline{58}\ \overline{59}$$

$10

$$\overline{60}\ \overline{61}\ \overline{62}\qquad \overline{63}\ \overline{64}\ \overline{65}\ \overline{66}\ \overline{67}\ \overline{68}\qquad \overline{69}\ \overline{70}\ \overline{71}\ \overline{72}$$

$20

$$\overline{73}\ \overline{74}\ \overline{75}\ \overline{76}\ \overline{77}\ \overline{78}\qquad \overline{79}\ \overline{80}\ \overline{81}\ \overline{82}\ \overline{83}\ \overline{84}\qquad \overline{85}\ \overline{86}\ \overline{87}\ \overline{88}$$

$50

$$\overline{89}\ \overline{90}\ \overline{91}\ \overline{92}\ \overline{93}\qquad \overline{94}\ \overline{95}\ \overline{96}\ \overline{97}\ \overline{98}\ \overline{99}\qquad \overline{100}\ \overline{101}\ \overline{102}\ \overline{103}$$

$$\overline{18}\qquad \overline{1}\ \overline{10}\ \overline{34}\ \overline{62}\ \overline{78}\qquad \overline{24}\ \overline{48}\ \overline{15}\ \overline{94}\qquad \overline{70}\qquad \overline{31}\qquad \overline{1}\ \overline{75}\ \overline{3}\ \overline{4}\ \overline{93}$$

$$\overline{61}\ \overline{67}\ \overline{99}\ \overline{76}\ \overline{35}\ \overline{50}$$

16

THE BUS STATION

DIRECTIONS: Put the cities in alphabetical order. Then write the correct letters in the numbered blanks at the bottom of the page.

You want to buy a bus ticket. Buses go to the following cities:

SAN ANTONIO	NEW YORK	DENVER
NEW ORLEANS	PITTSBURGH	LAS VEGAS
DALLAS	MIAMI	SAN FRANCISCO
PORTLAND	ATLANTA	BOSTON

1. $\underline{A}\ \underline{T}\ \underline{L}\ \underline{A}\ \underline{N}\ \underline{T}\ \underline{A}$
   ${7}{14}$

2. $\underline{}\ \underline{}\ \underline{}\ \underline{}\ \underline{}\ \underline{}$
   4

3. $\underline{}\ \underline{}\ \underline{}\ \underline{}\ \underline{}\ \underline{}$
   6

4. $\underline{}\ \underline{}\ \underline{}\ \underline{}\ \underline{}\ \underline{}$
   $18\ \ 10$

5. $\underline{}\ \underline{}\ \underline{}\quad\underline{}\ \underline{}\ \underline{}\ \underline{}$
   3

6. $\underline{}\ \underline{}\ \underline{}\ \underline{}\ \underline{}$
   $17\ \ 9$

7. $\underline{}\ \underline{}\ \underline{}\ \underline{}\quad\underline{}\ \underline{}\ \underline{}\ \underline{}\ \underline{}\ \underline{}$
   8

8. $\underline{}\ \underline{}\ \underline{}\quad\underline{}\ \underline{}\ \underline{}\ \underline{}$
   11

9. $\underline{}\ \underline{}\ \underline{}\ \underline{}\ \underline{}\ \underline{}\ \underline{}\ \underline{}\ \underline{}$
   $5\ \ \ 2$

10. $\underline{}\ \underline{}\ \underline{}\ \underline{}\ \underline{}\ \underline{}\ \underline{}$
    $13\ \ 15$

11. $\underline{}\ \underline{}\ \underline{}\quad\underline{}\ \underline{}\ \underline{}\ \underline{}\ \underline{}$
    1

12. $\underline{}\ \underline{}\ \underline{}\quad\underline{}\ \underline{}\ \underline{}\ \underline{}\ \underline{}\ \underline{}\ \underline{}$
    1216

$\overline{\ \ }\ \overline{\ \ }\ \overline{\ \ }\quad\overline{\ \ }\ \overline{\ \ }\ \overline{\ \ }\quad\overline{\ \ }\ \overline{\ \ }\ \overline{\ \ }\ \overline{\ \ }\ \overline{\ \ }\ \overline{\ \ }\quad\overline{\ \ }\ \overline{\ \ }\quad\overline{\ \ }\ \overline{\ \ }\ \overline{\ \ }\ \overline{\ \ }$!
$\ 1\ \ 2\ \ 3\quad\ 4\ \ 5\ \ 6\quad\ 7\ \ 8\ \ 9\ \ 10\ 11\ 12\quad 13\ 14\quad 15\ 16\ 17\ 18$

CARS

DIRECTIONS: Fill in the blanks with the correct words from the bottom of the page.

headlight

headlight	door	tire
roof	trunk	windshield
bumper	tail light	steering wheel
door handle	gas tank	hood

18

TWO-WORD VERBS

DIRECTIONS: Complete the sentences using the words below. (Note: Some words are used more than once.) Then fill in the numbered blanks at the bottom.

through   on   out   up   off   back   down   over   in

1. Cassy blew _u_ _p_ the balloon.

2. We sent __ __ __ __ the package.

     1

3. They tore __ __ __ __ the old building.

4. Jennifer likes to look __ __ __ __ __ __ __ catalogs.

         3

5. Walter blew __ __ __ the candles on his cake.

       7

6. Please stand __ __ straight.

7. They took __ __ __ __ their Christmas presents.

       6

8. Would you like to try __ __ the shoes?

9. He said to the gas station owner, "Fill 'er __ __ ."

10. Look __ __ the word in the dictionary.

11. Tear __ __ __ the top part of the page.

12. Bruce likes to try __ __ __ a car before he buys it.

        2

13. The Smiths came __ __ __ __ for dinner last night.

         5 4

14. The clerk took __ __ __ __ the information.

15. Hand __ __ your homework tomorrow.

__ __ __ __ __ __ __!
1 2 3 4 5 6 7

AT THE RESTAURANT

DIRECTIONS: Use the words at the bottom to fill in the crossword puzzle.

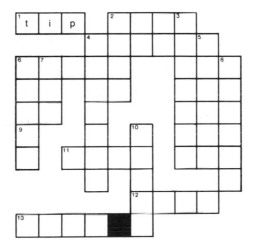

ACROSS

1. money given to the waiter

2. This coffee is _____ !

4. a drink

6. a kind of beef

11. list of food

12. person who makes the food

13. _____ and pepper

DOWN

2. short name for Coca-Cola™

3. ice cream, apple pie, etc.

4. person who takes the money

5. main dish

6. lettuce and tomato _____

7. a drink

8. person who takes your order

10. mid-day meal

cashier	dessert	salt
coffee	entree	steak
Coke	lunch	tea
cold	menu	tip
cook	salad	waiter

SIGNS

DIRECTIONS: Draw a line between the sign and the place where you would find it.

℞	movie theater	**eggs** 79¢/dozen
Lead-free $1.27/gal.	restaurant	*DON'T PICK THE FLOWERS*
ALL FLIGHTS ON TIME	drug store	LOT FILLED
FOR RENT	apartment	We have YOUR size!
Next feature: **10 P.M.**	airport	NOT FOR HIRE
QUIET PLEASE!	park	Exact Change only
SPEED LIMIT 55 MPH	gas station	OPEN FOR BREAKFAST *TRY OUR COFFEE*
U.S. MAIL	highway	

movie theater

restaurant

drug store

apartment

airport

park

gas station

highway

parking lot

supermarket

bus

shoe store

taxi

post office

library

ADJECTIVES

DIRECTIONS: Count the syllables in the underlined adjectives. Put the words into the right list at the bottom of the page.

Example: This is an <u>easy</u> book.   **Two syllables**

1. I live on the <u>fifth</u> floor.

2. He found the <u>secret</u> message.

3. My professor is very <u>intelligent</u>.

4. Today three students are <u>absent</u>.

5. There are twelve <u>underlined</u> words.

6. Students are always <u>busy</u>.

7. She sent a <u>registered</u> letter.

8. My grandfather is an <u>educated</u> man.

9. This shirt is <u>cheap</u>.

10. The letter was very <u>personal</u>.

11. These answers are <u>correct</u>.

12. The line is <u>horizontal</u>.

One Syllable	Two Syllables	Three Syllables	Four Syllables
1. _____	1. _easy_	1. _____	1. _____
2. _____	2. _____	2. _____	2. _____
	3. _____	3. _____	3. _____
	4. _____		

22

PAIRS

DIRECTIONS: Write a word in the blanks that makes a pair with the underlined word. Then fill in the numbered blanks at the bottom.

Example: I'll have <u>bacon</u> and <u>e</u> <u>g</u> <u>g</u> <u>s</u> .

1. Please pass the <u>salt</u> and __ __ __ __ __ .

                                    1

2. I have been <u>up</u> and __ __ __ __ the stairs a hundred times.

            2   3

3. She doesn't know <u>right</u> from __ __ __ __ __ .

                            4

4. The children were <u>in</u> and __ __ __ of the house all day.

5. He doesn't know his <u>left</u> hand from his __ __ __ __ __ __ .

                                      5

6. They fought like <u>cats</u> and __ __ __ __ .

                        6

7. They look like <u>brother</u> and __ __ __ __ __ __ .

8. The car cost an <u>arm</u> and a __ __ __ .

9. He walked <u>back</u> and __ __ __ __ __ all night.

                        7

10. Mr. and Mrs. Kent are just like my <u>aunt</u> and __ __ __ __ __ .

                                      8

11. That's the <u>long</u> and the __ __ __ __ __ of it.

12. He wants a new <u>ball</u> and __ __ __ .

                        9

13. I dropped my <u>knife</u> and __ __ __ __ .

14. They are as different as <u>night</u> and __ __ __ .

                              10 11 12

15. It's an <u>open</u> and __ __ __ __ case.

__ __ __ __   __ __ __   __ __ __ __ __!

7 5 3 1   9 4 2   6 11 8 10 12

ADVERBS

DIRECTIONS: Make ten sentences using phrases from groups A, B, and C.

Example: We worked slowly.

A	**B**	**C**
It	are going to arrive	late.
He	ate soup	quickly.
The teachers	rode the bicycles	easily.
I	like to read	slowly.
They	walked to the store	fast.
She	spoke French	quietly.
We	worked	loudly.
You	will play the piano	well.
The students	talk to everyone	badly.
You and I	are going to finish	early.

1. _____

2. _____

3. _____

4. _____

5. _____

6. _____

7. _____

8. _____

9. _____

10. _____

24

SCHEDULES

DIRECTIONS: Circle the letter of the correct choice. Then write the letters at the bottom.

First semester	
8:00	history
9:00	English
10:00	math

This is a _____ schedule.

   Q. library
   (R.) class
   S. museum

Today's Flights	
1 pm	Buffalo
2 pm	Toronto
3 pm	New York

This is a(n) _____ schedule.

   I. airline
   J. bus
   K. train

The Vikings	
Sat. March 10	Warriors
Sat. March 17	Hawks
Sat. March 24	Bears

This is a _____ schedule.

   E. zoo
   F. bus
   G. sports

Tuesday	
9 am	breakfast with Joe
10 am	meeting with Mr. Smith
noon	lunch with company president

This is a(n) _____ schedule.

   H. appointment
   I. class
   J. sports

The Blue Zephyr	
Lv.	8:32 am
Ar.	9:07 am — Fort Smith
Ar.	11:30 am — Little Rock

This is a(n) _____ schedule.

   T. train
   U. appointment
   V. doctor's

R _ _ _ _!

CROSSWORD VERBS

DIRECTIONS: Write the correct verb in the puzzle.

Example: Susie _____ pizza.
                    (like)

L	I	K	E	S

ACROSS

3. Don't _____ late tomorrow.
      (sleep)
5. We _____ the play last night.
      (understand)
6. Jesse forgot to _____ his homework.
                    (do)
7. Tom _____ his car every Saturday.
      (wash)
9. Six students _____ sick yesterday.
                  (be)
11. I _____ to the store tomorrow.
      (go)
13. John _____ the meeting early this morning.
        (leave)
14. They _____ home from school yesterday.
        (walk)
15. Rose _____ Spanish very well.
        (speak)

DOWN

1. Henry _____ German last year.
        (study)
2. Please _____ these numbers.
          (add)
4. Ann _____ piano every day.
        (practice)
8. Don't _____ late for class tomorrow.
          (be)
12. She _____ ten years old last week.
          (be)

BACKWARD/FORWARD WORDS

DIRECTIONS: Some words are written the same backward and forward. Draw a line from the definition at the left to the correct word on the right.

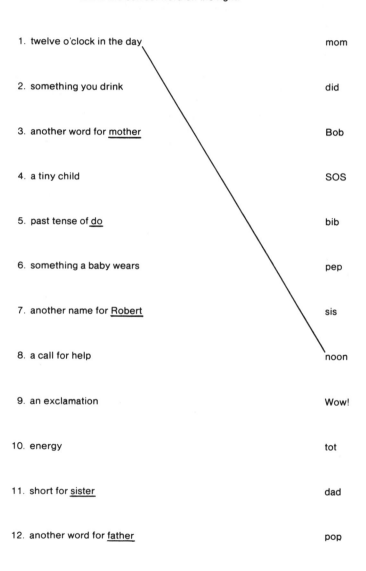

1. twelve o'clock in the day	mom
2. something you drink	did
3. another word for <u>mother</u>	Bob
4. a tiny child	SOS
5. past tense of <u>do</u>	bib
6. something a baby wears	pep
7. another name for <u>Robert</u>	sis
8. a call for help	noon
9. an exclamation	Wow!
10. energy	tot
11. short for <u>sister</u>	dad
12. another word for <u>father</u>	pop

THE MOVIES

DIRECTIONS: Unscramble the sentences. Rewrite them on the lines at the bottom of the page.

Example: like / do you / movies   Do you like movies?

1. to the movies / to go / everyone likes

2. different kinds / of movies / people prefer

3. Westerns / likes / my father

4. mysteries / my mother / likes

5. prefers / my brother / science fiction

6. my sister / love stories / chooses

7. always wants / monster movies / my best friend / to see

8. go / my other friends / to comedies

9. to everything / go / I

10. the popcorn / love / I

1. _____

2. _____

3. _____

4. _____

5. _____

6. _____

7. _____

8. _____

9. _____

10. _____

TELEVISION

DIRECTIONS: Find the following words in the puzzle. Circle them.

antenna ✓	games	sports
black and white	movies	television
cartoons	news	TV set
channel	program	UHF
color	soap opera	weather

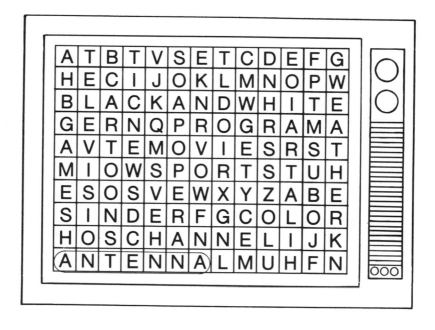

FAST FOOD AND SNACKS

DIRECTIONS: Unscramble the letters to make a word. Write the word in the blank.

Example: A __snack__ is something eaten between meals.
                    kasnc

Americans are always in a hurry. Sometimes for breakfast they eat

_____ and _____ or instant _____ .
      studno   feefoc   acerel

At lunch they sometimes have _____ or _____
                                          oth sodg   srebmarugh

and _____ . Instant _____ is eaten too.
       chenfr risef   opsu

Sometimes for dinner they order _____ or _____ .
                                              pizaz   ridef neckich

Other times they cook a _____ .
                                VT nidren

Americans like to have snacks, too. At movies they buy _____ ,
                                                                  ydanc

_____ , and _____ . Watching television, they sometimes have
      norpcop   tofs nirdsk

_____ or _____ .
   atpoto spich   zepsletr

THE POST OFFICE

DIRECTIONS: Match the first part of each sentence with the second part. Draw a line between them. Then rewrite the sentences at the bottom of the page.

1. I went to the post office.   very long.

2. I also wanted to buy   the package first class.

3. The line was   home slowly.

4. But it moved   was closed.

5. I sent   to mail a package.

6. The cost was   something.

7. I walked   buy the stamps.

8. Then I remembered   very quickly.

9. I forgot to $2.40.

10. When I returned, the post office   some stamps.

1. _I went to the post office to mail a package._

2. _____

3. _____

4. _____

5. _____

6. _____

7. _____

8. _____

9. _____

10. _____

MUSIC! MUSIC! MUSIC!

DIRECTIONS: Make new words from the words below.

Example: **SONG**

no
go
so

RADIO

STEREO

RECORD

SPEAKERS

CASSETTE TAPE

HEADPHONES

32

AT THE BANK

DIRECTIONS: Put the following sentences in order to make a story. Then write the story in the blanks which are below the sentences.

He gave me twenties and tens.

I stood in line for fifteen minutes.

She helped me open a savings account.

Yesterday I went to the bank. 1

The officer gave me a free gift for opening the account.

I asked the teller to cash my check.

Then I went to speak to one of the officers.

I'll go again next week.

1. Yesterday I went to the bank. _____

2. _____

3. _____

4. _____

5. _____

6. _____

7. _____

8. _____

COLORS

DIRECTIONS: Unscramble the letters to make a word. Write the word in the blank.

Example: Fire engines are ___red___.
erd

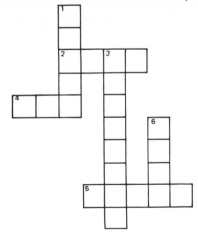

1. Zebras are _____ and _____.
kacbl   tewih

2. _____ roses are my favorite flowers.
weloly

3. Grass is _____ in the summer.
nereg

4. I like your new _____ shoes.
worbn

5. Susan has _____ eyes.
uleb

6. Mark drives an _____ car.
regona

7. His _____ hair is short.
yarg

IRREGULAR PLURALS

DIRECTIONS: Write the plurals of the following words in the blanks. Then write the words in the puzzle.

Example: leaf ___leaves___

1. woman _____

2. mouse _____

3. child _____

4. man _____

5. tooth _____

6. foot _____

DAYS AND MONTHS

DIRECTIONS: Find the seven days of the week and the twelve months of the year in the puzzle and circle them.

```
C D E F Y X Y Z B H R
O R A B A P Q R S T Q
C Y M E D F G D O G P
Y R A U N A J E C F O
A A R J U N E C T C V
U U C N S O A E O D M
G R H Y B V Z M B E F
U B A N A E Y B E A R
S E P T E M B E R W P
T F R K C B O R I V O
A T I L D E Y N J U Q
J U L Y X R A H D K M
W E D N E S D A Y A L
B S D S I T I G W K Y
O D E T H U R S D A Y
P A F R J U F H V L S
Q Y A D R U T A S M T
```

APRIL MONDAY JANUARY WEDNESDAY AUGUST THURSDAY

FEBRUARY MAY FRIDAY DECEMBER

SEPTEMBER SATURDAY JULY NOVEMBER

OCTOBER SUNDAY JUNE TUESDAY MARCH

GROCERIES

DIRECTIONS: Fill in the blanks with the word that matches the picture. Then write the correct letters in the numbered blanks at the bottom of the page.

SHOPPING LIST

c	h	e	e	s	e
1	11	21	31	41	47

__	__	__	__
2	12	22	32

__	__	__	__
3	13	23	33

__	__	__	__
4	14	24	34

__	__	__	__	__	__	__
5	15	25	35	42	48	52

__	__	__	__	__	__	__
6	16	26	36	43	49	53

__	__	__	__	__
7	17	27	37	44

__	__	__	__	__	__	__
8	18	28	38	45	50	54

__	__	__	__	__	__
9	19	29	39	46	51

__	__	__	__
10	20	30	40

__	__	__	__		__	__	__
39	21	49	33		40	9	49

CONTRACTIONS

DIRECTIONS: Fill in the blanks with the contraction of the underlined words. Then read the hidden word above the arrow.

Example: <u>He</u> <u>is</u> a student. | H | E' | S |

He <u>can</u> <u>not</u> sing.

I <u>do</u> <u>not</u> like pizza.

It <u>is</u> <u>not</u> humid today.

She <u>does</u> not want coffee.

<u>We</u> <u>are</u> close friends.

<u>What</u> <u>is</u> his name?

They <u>could</u> <u>not</u> do the problem.

<u>They</u> <u>are</u> cousins.

<u>I</u> <u>am</u> tired.

<u>You</u> <u>are</u> a good dancer.

We <u>are</u> <u>not</u> hungry.

<u>Who</u> <u>is</u> the new student?

↑
hidden word

BODY PARTS

DIRECTIONS: Fill in the blanks with the correct words.

News Flash!! A spaceship landed today.
This is a picture of the pilot.

He has a square __head__ .

His _____ are closed.

He has two _____ .

He has long _____ .

His _____ are thin.

His _____ are big.

He has a round _____ .

His _____ are small.

His _____ is short.

His _____ each have

six _____ .

He has a flower on

his _____ .

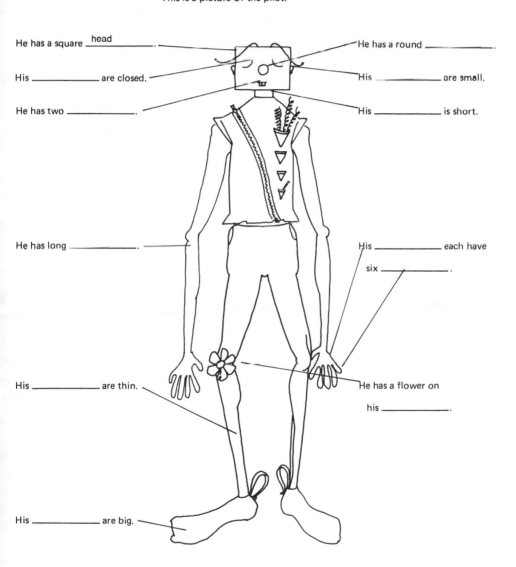

38

FURNITURE

DIRECTIONS: Fill in the blanks with the words at the bottom of the page to find the hidden word above the arrow that describes them all.

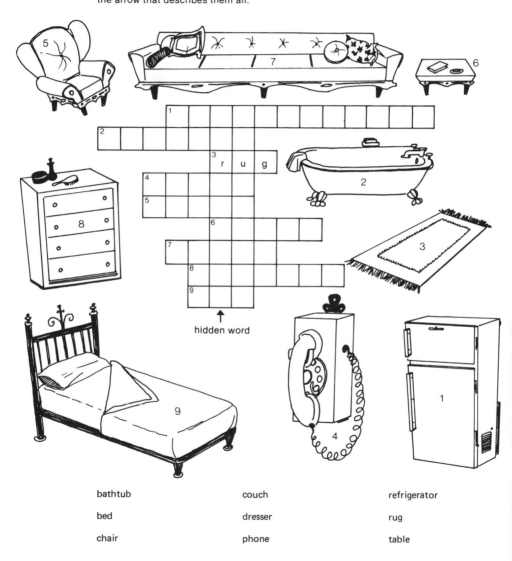

3 r u g

hidden word

bathtub	couch	refrigerator
bed	dresser	rug
chair	phone	table

FAMILY

DIRECTIONS: Look at the family tree. Then read the paragraph and fill in the blanks correctly. Names of family members are given below the family tree.

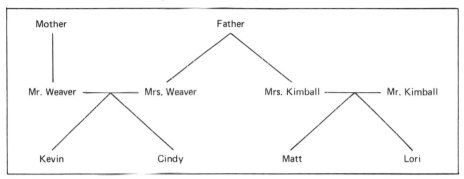

Family members: husband, wife, son, daughter, aunt, uncle, sister, brother, cousins, grandfather, grandmother, father

Mr. and Mrs. Weaver are married. They have two children, a boy, Kevin, and a girl, Cindy. Kevin is Mr. and Mrs. Weaver's _____son_____. Cindy is their _____. Cindy is Kevin's _____. Kevin is Cindy's _____. Mr. Weaver's mother lives with the Weavers. She is Kevin and Cindy's _____. Mrs. Weaver's sister, Mrs. Kimball, sometimes brings her family to visit the Weavers. Mrs. Kimball is married to Mr. Kimball. He is her _____. She is his _____. Mr. and Mrs. Kimball also have two children, a boy, Matt, and a girl, Lori. Mrs. Weaver is Matt and Lori's _____. Mr. Weaver is their _____. Mrs. Kimball is Kevin and Cindy's _____. Mr. Kimball is their _____. Cindy and Kevin are Matt and Lori's _____. Lori is Matt's _____. Matt is Lori's _____. Sometimes Mrs. Kimball brings her father to the Weavers' house. Mrs. Kimball's father is also Mrs. Weaver's _____. He is the _____ of all four children.

We are different things to different people.

HOME ACTIVITIES

DIRECTIONS: Look at the picture. Fill in the blanks with the correct form of the verbs at the bottom of the page.

Example: The dog _____is eating_____ his food.

It's Saturday. The Schultz family is at home. Everyone is doing something. Mrs. Schultz

_____ the piano in the living room, and Grandpa _____ TV.

In the kitchen, Maria _____, and Peter _____ the dishes.

Mr. Schultz _____ the garage. Grandma _____ her hair in the

bathroom. The baby _____ in the bedroom.

brush	eat	sit
clean	listen	sleep
cook	play	wash
drink	read	watch

SEASONS AND WEATHER

DIRECTIONS: Find the underlined words in the puzzle.

Alice: What's the <u>weather</u> like today?

Karen: It's <u>cloudy</u> and <u>cold</u>. I think it's going to <u>snow</u>.

Alice: Good. I like <u>winter</u>.

Karen: I don't. I like <u>spring</u>. Then it's <u>windy</u> and <u>rainy</u>. I love <u>summer</u>, too. Then it's <u>hot</u> and <u>sunny</u>.

Alice: My favorite <u>season</u> is fall. Sometimes it's <u>foggy</u> in the morning, but the days are always <u>mild</u>.

```
S N O W A B D X
L J S P R I N G
G R E M M U S W
W E A T H E R I
D H S U N N Y N
L F O G G Y N D
O A N T Y C I Y
C L O U D Y A H
D L I M Z E R I
F W I N T E R K
```

NUMBERS

DIRECTIONS: Fill in the puzzle with the correct answers.

Example: Two plus two | F | O | U | R |

Across

1. fifty divided by twenty-five
4. seven times two
5. eleven times three
9. thirty-two divided by four
11. eighty-three minus thirteen
13. eighteen minus nine
14. three times five

Down

1. nine times three
2. ninety-two minus fifty-two
3. one hundred minus ninety-nine
6. thirty-seven plus thirteen
7. fifteen times four
8. fifty-four plus twenty-six
10. thirty-six divided by three
12. six plus four

$$3 \overline{)93} \quad \text{(quotient 31)}$$

$$3 \times 31 = 93$$

$$\begin{array}{r} 96 \\ -3 \\ \hline 93 \end{array} \qquad \begin{array}{r} 90 \\ +3 \\ \hline 93 \end{array}$$

CLOTHES

DIRECTIONS: Circle the word that does <u>not</u> belong with the others. Write each circled word in the blanks below. Then fill in the blanks at the bottom of the page with the correct letters.

Example: dog   cat   bird   (car)

1. coat   watch   gloves   boots

2. tie   skirt   blouse   dress

3. ice skates   golf shoes   umbrella   tennis shoes

4. pants   shirt   tie   dress

5. sweater   purse   jacket   raincoat

6. shoes   socks   hat   boots

7. watch   bracelet   ring   socks

8. fan   pants   shorts   jeans

1. __ __ __ __ __ __ __
   49 41 33 25 17 9   1

2. __ __ __ __ __ __
   50 42 34 26 18 10 2

3. __ __ __ __ __ __ __ __ __ __ __ __
   62 61 60 58 55 51 43 35 27 19 11 3

4. __ __ __ __ __ __
   44 36 28 20 12 4

5. __ __ __ __ __ __ __ __
   56 52 45 37 29 21 13 5

6. __ __ __ __ __ __
   46 38 30 22 14 6

7. __ __ __ __ __ __ __ __ __
   59 57 53 47 39 31 23 15 7

8. __ __ __ __ __ __ __
   54 48 40 32 24 16 8

__ __ __ __ __ __ __ __ __ __ __ __ __ __ __ __ .
33 46 29   25 51 57 20 34 50   42 12   54 62 51 43

44

PAIRS

DIRECTIONS: Write in the blanks a word that makes a pair with the underlined word.

Example: He has a new <u>ball</u> and <u>b</u> <u>a</u> <u>t</u>.

1. The <u>cup</u> and __ __ __ __ __ are broken.

2. I'll have <u>bacon</u> and __ __ __ __.

3. Pass the <u>bread</u> and __ __ __ __ __ __.

4. Mom wants a new dining room <u>table</u> and __ __ __ __ __ __.

5. My <u>shoes</u> and __ __ __ __ __ are under the bed.

6. He likes <u>ham</u> and __ __ __ __ for breakfast.

7. I take <u>cream</u> and __ __ __ __ __ in my coffee.

8. He forgot his <u>hat</u> and __ __ __ __.

9. The cabin has <u>hot</u> and __ __ __ __ __ running water.

10. Sam and Helen are __ __ __ __ __ __ __ and <u>wife</u>.

11. I forgot to pack my <u>brush</u> and __ __ __ __.

12. Waiter, please bring me a __ __ __ __ __ __ and <u>fork</u>.

OPPOSITES

DIRECTIONS: Write in the blanks a word that is the opposite of the word at the left. Then read the hidden message above the arrow.

Example: come | G | O |

ceiling
sad
absent
behind
hard (test)
big
before
goodbye
a little of
right
midnight
clean
night
open

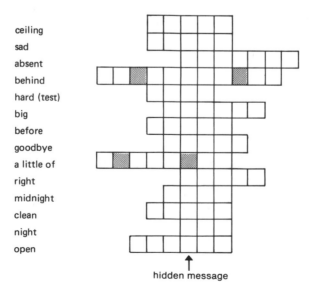

hidden message

45

VERBS WITH TIME EXPRESSIONS

DIRECTIONS: Fill in the blanks with the correct form of the verb in parentheses. Then fill in the blanks at the bottom of the page with the correct letters.

Example: My brother _l_ _i_ _k_ _e_ _s_ baseball. (like)

1. Carl usually _ _ _ _ _ _ the questions correctly. (answer)
   1

2. I _ _ _ _ _ our new car yesterday. (wash)
   3

3. Will you _ _ _ _ _ _ my apology? (accept)
   13

4. My brother _ _ _ _ _ _ _ _ piano every day. (practice)
   4

5. They _ _ _ _ _ _ _ _ at the university next year. (study)
   5

6. My sister sometimes _ _ _ _ _ _ she is wrong. (admit)
   6

7. Did you _ _ _ _ your hair this morning? (comb)
   14

8. Last night we all _ _ _ _ _ _ _ the football game. (watch)
   7

9. Tomorrow I _ _ _ _ _ _ _ _ my new outfit. (wear)
   8   15

10. My father never _ _ _ _ _ _ an umbrella. (carry)
    16

11. He _ _ _ _ _ _ the neighbors last week. (help)
    17

12. Do you _ _ _ _ _ with me? (agree)
    10

13. They _ _ _ _ _ _ _ _ _ _ _ _ their anniversary next month. (celebrate)
    11   18

14. Olga _ _ _ _ _ to help her mother every day. (try)
    19   12

15. Edison _ _ _ _ _ _ _ _ the light bulb. (invent)
    2   9

_ _ _ _ _ _ _ _ _ _ _ _ _ _ _ _ _ _ _!
1 2 3 4 5 6 7 8 9 10 11 12 13 14 15 16 17 18 19

SCHOOL

DIRECTIONS: Unscramble the letters to make a word.

Example: I was late for _____class_____ today.
                                   slacs

1. The _____ picks me up at 7:30 every morning.
       sub verird

2. My first class is _____. The _____ gives a lot of _____.
               shiglen   cehaetr   snetmsagins

3. Then I have gym class. _____ is my favorite sport.
                         crocse

4. Before lunch I have _____ and _____. The first is interesting, but the other
                    atemhicstam   ortshiy

    is _____.
       binorg

6. After lunch, I have _____ class. Last week I forgot my _____ paper.
             cenesic   morekohw

    The teacher gave me two extra _____.
                               sixersece

6. I work in the _____ the last hour of the day.
          rabrily

7. Some days after school I go to the _____ to buy _____
                          obsetrook   tookbones

    and _____. Other days my _____ and I _____ soccer.
          sincelp   metscasals   catprice

Note: Did you remember capital letters?!

OCCUPATIONS

DIRECTIONS: Read the descriptions below and fill in the crossword puzzle.

	Across	*Down*
	One who:	One who:
	3. delivers packages	1. works with electricity
	6. plans meals	2. keeps accounts
	10. helps when you are sick	4. plans buildings
	11. builds houses	5. takes pictures
	12. paints	7. works on a farm
	13. treats teeth	8. sells things
	14. delivers milk	9. writes for a newspaper
	15. works in a garden	

3 across filled in: d e l i v e r y m a n

SIGNS

DIRECTIONS: Draw a line between the sign and its meaning.

picnic area

stop

railroad crossing

yield

no smoking

pedestrian crossing

handicapped

no left turn

telephone

school crossing

go

no animals

poisonous

ladies' room

men's room

FOLLOWING DIRECTIONS

DIRECTIONS: Follow the directions below the map. Answer the questions that follow. Then fill in the last blanks at the bottom. Are you correct?

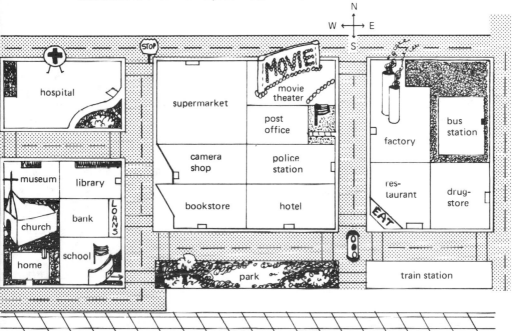

Start at school. Walk north. Turn right at the first corner. Walk two blocks and turn left. Go into the first building. When you come out, walk north again. Turn left at the first corner. Turn left at the next corner. Go into the second building on your right. When you come out, walk south. Turn right at the first corner. Go into the second building on your right. When you come out, continue to your right. Turn left at the first corner. Then turn right at the next corner. Go into the second building on your right.

Which buildings did you go into?

d r u g s t o r e
1 2 3 4 5 6 7 8 9

— — — — — — — — — —
10 11 12 13 14 15 16 17 18 19

— — — — — — — — —
20 21 22 23 24 25 26 27 28

Where are you now?

— — — —
29 30 31 32

— — — — —!
2 17 4 29 6

PRODUCTS AND STORES

DIRECTIONS: Match each store with a product you can buy there. Write the correct letter in the blank next to the store.

Example: __Z__ shoe store   Z. shoes

1. ____ supermarket	A. stamps
2. ____ bookstore	B. camera
3. ____ drugstore	C. chair
4. ____ post office	D. watch
5. ____ photo supply store	E. brush
6. ____ hardware store	F. bread
7. ____ paint store	G. aspirin
8. ____ candy store	H. books
9. ____ jewelry store	I. meat
10. ____ sporting goods store	J. hammer
11. ____ furniture store	K. chocolate
12. ____ bakery	L. basketball

HOLIDAYS

DIRECTIONS: Circle the word or words that do not belong with the others.

Example: Christmas   December   tree   (hot dogs)

1. New Year's   midnight   money   party
2. February   animals   Valentine's Day   cards
3. Irish   purple   March   St. Patrick's Day
4. fireworks   July Fourth   picnics   gifts
5. June   Halloween   costumes   pumpkins
6. office   Thanksgiving   family   turkey
7. flowers   May   Mother's Day   red
8. tricks   April Fool's Day   vacation   April
9. Easter   church   eggs   snow

SPORTS

DIRECTIONS: Match each sport with the correct equipment for it. Draw a line from the name of the sport to the picture.

football   volleyball

basketball   track

tennis   swimming

baseball   roller-skating

golf   ice-skating

soccer   boxing

hockey   fishing

ping pong   gymnastics

racquetball   diving

badminton   skiing

IRREGULAR PAST TENSE

DIRECTIONS: Write the correct form of the verb in parentheses in the blank. Then look for your answer in the puzzle and circle it.

Example: My brother _____slept_____ late this morning.
(sleep)

1. I _____ her a letter last week.
(write)

2. The old man _____ stories about his home last night.
(tell)

3. My friend and I _____ to the movies yesterday.
(go)

4. Herb _____ a bad grade on his last report card.
(get)

5. Tom _____ coffee with his donut this morning.
(drink)

6. She _____ me her telephone number again.
(give)

7. We _____ the directions that he sent.
(understand)

8. Rosa _____ a toothache last night.
(have)

9. The students _____ late to class yesterday.
(come)

10. I _____ too much this morning.
(eat)

11. She _____ quietly when they called.
(speak)

12. Ken _____ all the answers last week.
(know)

13. We _____ the Abominable Snowman last winter.
(see)

14. The class _____ early today.
(begin)

15. Rita _____ the wrong page yesterday.
(do)

```
U Z D O T U N H L M
A N I K P S G A V E
B Y D N Q R X D K M
F A T E T O R W J A
C M L W R K J I W C
D W V U P S N O E I
E R S T Q P T A N T
F H G S F O G O T O
G D R A N K C B O L
H E D W B E G A N D
```

TRANSPORTATION

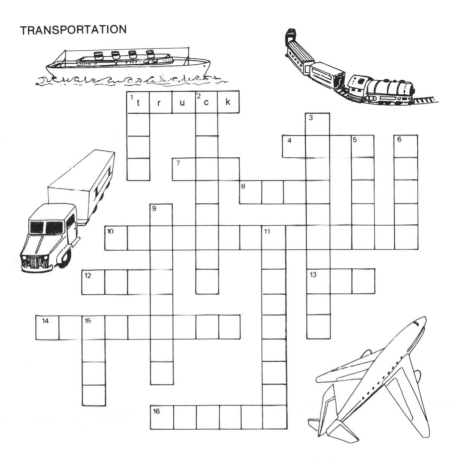

Across

1. vehicle that carries things (larger than a car)
4. something to go fishing in
7. transportation to school
8. another word for car
10. permit to drive
12. transportation across the ocean
13. Ford is a kind of _____.
14. emergency vehicle
16. place to park a car

Down

1. vehicle that has a meter
2. person who drives a limousine
3. two-wheeled vehicle with a motor
5. vehicle that runs on tracks
6. animal used for transportation
9. vehicle that flies
11. wealthy person's car
15. vehicle with two wheels

54

ENGLISH-SPEAKING COUNTRIES

DIRECTIONS: Unscramble the letters to make names of English-speaking countries. Then put the names in the puzzle.

1. ewn ezdanal   New Zealand
2. lerinad
3. daanac
4. nalcstod
5. gelnand
6. atrusaali
7. sua
8. adini

Note: Did you remember capital letters?!

TWO-WORD VERBS

DIRECTIONS: Fill in the blanks with an appropriate word from the bottom of the page. Then write the word in the puzzle. You will have to use some words more than once. The arrow points to a hidden description of these words.

Example: Turn ____off____ the radio. | O | F | F |

1. Please fill _____ the application.
2. Sit _____.
3. Would you turn _____ the lights?
4. Write _____ the words when I say them.
5. Why don't you take _____ your coat?
6. Follow _____ with your ideas.
7. Peggy turned Mark _____ for a date.
8. Look _____ your answers.
9. Come _____ at 7 o'clock.
10. Did you look _____ the book?
11. Why don't you come _____ for dinner tonight?

down	out
for	over
off	through
on	back

hidden description

GOOD, BETTER, BEST

DIRECTIONS: Fill in the blanks with the correct form of the word in parentheses. Then write the numbered letters in the puzzle.

Example: Sears Tower is the <u>t</u> <u>a</u> <u>l</u> <u>l</u> <u>e</u> <u>s</u> <u>t</u> building in the world. (tall)

1. Rocky is the __ __ __ __ __ __ __ __ man in the world. (strong)
                 1   2 3

2. That dog is the __ __ __ __ __ __ pet we've ever had. (bad)
            4   5

3. Mrs. Allen has the __ __ __ __ __ __ __ __ house in town. (clean)
             6   7 8 9

4. He's the __ __ __ __ __ __ __ man in the country. (rich)
         15   16 17

5. This is the __ __ __ __ car I've ever had. (good)
         18 19   20

Example: Are you __ __ __ __ __ __ than your wife? (busy)

6. Is Laura __ __ __ __ __ __ __ than her sister? (thin)
         10 11 12 13   14

7. She is __ __ __ __ __ __ __ than she looks. (young)
       24   21   22 23

8. This summer is __ __ __ __ __ than last summer. (dry)
        25

9. This car is __ __ __ __ __ __ __ __ __ __ than the other. (valuable)
       26   27   28

	25	1	8	10		18	22	6	12	17	27	19			
3	27	14	23	24	20	16	15	13	2		24	26	21	11	28	7	5

DRUGSTORE

DIRECTIONS: Unscramble the letters to make words that complete the paragraph. Write each word in the blank.

Example: Let's go to the _____drugstore_____.
rudgortes

In the United States, many things are sold in a drugstore. If your friend has a birthday,

you can buy a _____. If you want to know the date, you can buy a
hitrabdy drac

_____. If you want to read, you can buy _____,
rencalda   omcic sobok

_____, and _____. If you're hungry, you can buy
sagemazin   rewnsseppa

_____ or _____. If you want to write a friend, you can
dynca   cei merca

get a _____ or some _____. If you want to listen to
dorscapt   penosveel

music, you can look for a _____. If you want to get up on time, get an
coderr

_____. If you need change, ask the _____. Sometimes
ralam lokcc   chirase

there is a _____, and you can buy things very _____.
laes   lpeachy

If you have a headache, you can even buy _____ at the drugstore.
pinsira

TOOLS

DIRECTIONS: Make as many new words as you can from the letters in the words below. Write your new words in the blanks.

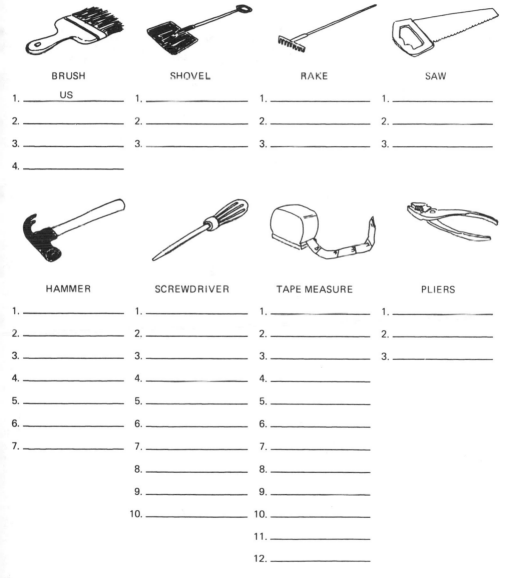

BRUSH	SHOVEL	RAKE	SAW
1. __US__	1. _____	1. _____	1. _____
2. _____	2. _____	2. _____	2. _____
3. _____	3. _____	3. _____	3. _____
4. _____			

HAMMER	SCREWDRIVER	TAPE MEASURE	PLIERS
1. _____	1. _____	1. _____	1. _____
2. _____	2. _____	2. _____	2. _____
3. _____	3. _____	3. _____	3. _____
4. _____	4. _____	4. _____	
5. _____	5. _____	5. _____	
6. _____	6. _____	6. _____	
7. _____	7. _____	7. _____	
	8. _____	8. _____	
	9. _____	9. _____	
	10. _____	10. _____	
		11. _____	
		12. _____	

IRREGULAR PAST PARTICIPLES

DIRECTIONS: Complete the sentences with the correct form of an appropriate verb from those listed at the bottom of the page. Some words may be used more than once.

Example: Has Chuck _____fallen_____ asleep again?

1.   Have you _____ today's newspaper? The rock group Soul has _____ a new record. They have _____ their newest song every night at their concerts. Fans have _____ in line for hours to buy tickets and have _____ $10 each for them. Have you _____ any?

2.   I've _____ my gloves. Have you _____ them? I hope so. They're my best pair. I've _____ them every day this winter.

3.   My sister has _____ too much time to be with her boyfriend. She's really _____ behind in her studies.

4.   My aunt has _____ in an airplane many times, but she's _____ nervous every time. She has _____ magazines to read. She has _____ her prayers. She has _____ the curtains on the window. She has _____ talking to the person in the next seat. Nothing has worked.

5.   Greg has _____ to set his alarm every day this week. He has _____ late every day.

be	fly	pay	sleep
bring	forget	read	stand
buy	keep	say	take
fall	lose	shut	wear
find	make	sing	

SOCIAL LIFE

DIRECTIONS: Find the underlined words in the puzzle and circle them.

Michelle is going to give a <u>party</u> after the basketball <u>game</u> on Friday night. She has invited <u>thirty</u> <u>classmates</u>. She is planning to serve <u>pizza</u>. Her brother said she could borrow his <u>stereo</u>. Rita will bring her <u>records</u>, and Mike is going to bring his tape <u>recorder</u> and his best <u>tape</u>. Flora might bring her <u>guitar</u>. Most of the students will <u>dance</u>. No one is coming with a <u>date</u>. Since Tony has his <u>license</u> and a <u>car</u>, he can <u>drive</u> some of the students to Michelle's.

```
M F D P I N L G C R A
S C L A S S M A T E S
T H I R T Y H M O C R
O A C T D E E E E O A
R Z E Y G P R C A R T
J Z N K A E V I R D I
P I S T T D A N C E U
B P E S D R O C E R G
```

60

NEWSPAPER ADS

DIRECTIONS: Replace the shortened forms of words underlined with the words they stand for. Then fill in the blanks at the bottom of the page.

Example: Everything 4 sale. $\underline{f}\ \underline{o}\ \underline{r}$

FOR SALE

8 rm. hse. w/4 BRs, brkfst. rm., & fam. rm. w/frplc.
3000 sq. ft. 2 car gar. Near shopping ctr. and trans.
$70,000

FOR RENT

4 rm. apt. w/wshr. & dryer. Crpt. in liv. rm. & BR.
1st flr w/storage in bsmt.
$250/mo.

```
___ ___ ___          ___ ___ ___ ___          ___ ___ ___          ___ ___ ___ ___ ___ ___ ___ ___
 2                    11                        13                   22

___ ___ ___          ___ ___ ___ ___ ___ ___ ___          ___ ___ ___ ___ ___          ___ ___ ___ ___ ___
24 31                 21                                    28                           23     18

___ ___ ___          ___ ___ ___ ___ ___          ___ ___ ___ ___ ___
 27                   8                            1

___ ___ ___ ___ ___ ___ ___          ___ ___ ___ ___ ___ ___
 26                                    14

___ ___ ___ ___ ___          ___ ___ ___ ___
                             16

___ ___ ___ ___ ___          ___ ___ ___ ___ ___          ___ ___ ___ ___ ___ ___
 17                           5                             9

___ ___ ___ ___ ___ ___ ___ ___ ___ ___          ___ ___ ___ ___ ___
                                               30            19
```

WANTED

Bldg. 15 min. N. of town for store. Call 555-1234
days or eve.

FOR SALE

1970 Ford. 4 dr. sdn. 50,000 mi. 15 mpg. A/c.
New tires. Best offer.

```
___ ___ ___ ___ ___ ___ ___          ___ ___ ___ ___
                 6                     3

___ ___ ___ ___ ___ ___ ___          ___ ___ ___ ___
              25                        7

___ ___ ___ ___ ___          ___ ___ ___ ___ / ___ ___ ___ / ___ ___ ___ ___ ___ ___
           10                           15                                        20

___ ___ ___ ___ ___ ___          ___ ___ / ___ ___ ___ ___ ___ ___ ___ ___
            29                          12                                4
```

```
___ ___ ___   ___ ___ ___ ___ ___   ___ ___ ___ ___ ___ ___ ___ ___ ___
 8 30 13     23  7 12 26  1 19 3     17 5  8 25 28 29 20 4

___ ___   ___ ___ ___ ___   ___ ___ ___ ___ ___ ___ ___ ___ ___.
31  6     16 10 15 27      11 24 21 22  9 18 14  2
```

Name _____ Date _____ Master 29

EXPRESSIONS

DIRECTIONS: Fill in the blanks with a word which will complete the common expression in each sentence.

Example: They are as different as n i g h t and day.

1. The Smiths fight like cats and _ _ _ _.

2. I looked high and _ _ _ for my camera.

3. Traffic at rush hour is always _ _ _ _ and go.

4. They mix like oil and _ _ _ _ _ _.

5. He walked _ _ _ _ and forth all evening.

6. They will stay together through thick and _ _ _ _ _.

7. The kids ran in and _ _ _ of the house all day.

8. I walked up and _ _ _ _ _ those stairs fifty times yesterday.

9. He gave money away right and _ _ _ _.

10. It's a give and _ _ _ _ _ situation.

11. That's the long and the _ _ _ _ _ _ of it.

12. They come and _ _ _ whenever they want.

FEELINGS

DIRECTIONS: Make as many new words as you can from letters in the words below.

BORED	INTERESTED	ANGRY	PLEASED	WORRIED
1. ___ or ___	1. _____	1. _____	1. _____	1. _____
2. _____	2. _____	2. _____	2. _____	2. _____
3. _____	3. _____	3. _____	3. _____	3. _____
4. _____	4. _____	4. _____	4. _____	4. _____
5. _____	5. _____	5. _____	5. _____	5. _____
6. _____	6. _____	6. _____	6. _____	6. _____

JOB HUNTING

DIRECTIONS: Use the clues below to fill in the crossword puzzle.

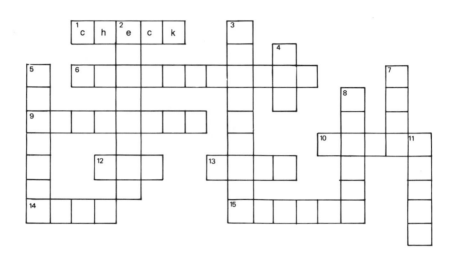

Across

1. On payday you get a _____.
6. the form you fill out to get a job
9. the person you work for
10. The day I was born is my _____ date.
12. male/female
13. another word meaning "to employ"
14. "I can't work nights, but I can work _____."
15. 157 lbs.

Down

2. one who works for another
3. a meeting with an employer before you get a job
4. another word for work
5. Saturday and Sunday
7. "I can't work full time, but I can work _____ time."
8. 5'9"
11. 4 pm–8 pm daily

OTHER WAYS OF SAYING THINGS I

DIRECTIONS: For each sentence find the word(s) from the list at the bottom of the page that means almost the same thing as the underlined word(s). Write your answers in the blanks at the left.

got out of   1. He <u>left</u> the burning building in a hurry.

_____ 2. Did Randy <u>telephone you</u>?

_____ 3. You'll <u>improve</u> fast with medicine.

_____ 4. She <u>returned</u> to work.

_____ 5. Please <u>complete</u> the form.

_____ 6. The detective <u>searched</u> every room in the house.

_____ 7. She <u>entered</u> the taxi gracefully.

_____ 8. Grandmother <u>became ill</u>.

call you up	got in
fill out	got out of
get better	got sick
went back	looked through

OTHER WAYS OF SAYING THINGS II

DIRECTIONS: For each sentence find the word(s) from the list at the bottom of the page that means almost the same thing as the underlined word(s). Write your answers in the blanks at the left.

_____ 1. <u>Give me a ring</u> the next time you're in town.

_____ 2. <u>Drop me a line</u> when you have time.

_____ 3. I'm <u>beat</u>!

_____ 4. Do you <u>give up</u>?

_____ 5. I'm going to <u>look him up</u> when I'm in New York.

_____ 6. <u>Drop in</u> about six o'clock.

call me up	quit
come over	very tired
contact him	write me

EMERGENCIES

DIRECTIONS: Fill in the blanks to complete the paragraph. Then find the answers in the puzzle and circle them.

Example: An ___ambulance___ will take him to the hospital.

In case of emergency, you can rely on many people in the community for _____. For example, if you have a toothache, you can call the _____. If you fall down and think your leg is _____, you can call the _____. If you see a fire, first shout _____! Then call the fire _____. If you see a car hit another car, call the _____ to report the _____. You may even have to call the _____ to get an ambulance. The important thing is to get to a _____ as quickly as possible. If there is no telephone _____, you can call the _____ for help. Don't forget the people that live near you. _____ can always help.

```
D N O H B P M I E A
D E P A R T M E N T
F I E L O V R Q N S
I G R S K P L E H I
R H A W E X D Y N T
E B T O N I U T J N
B O O K C P H O N E
K R R C R O T C O D
G S A P O L I C E B
C H O S P I T A L F
```

ANSWER KEY

Page 1: WHO AM I?

1. teacher
2. barber
3. fire fighter
4. garbage collector
5. mail carrier
6. policeman
7. dentist
8. doctor
9. farmer
10. cook

Page 2: RIDDLES

1. pan
2. dish
3. tub
4. car
5. pen
6. toy
7. mop
8. lamp
9. book
10. cat
11. dog
12. house
13. coat
14. pool
15. milk

Page 3: PREPOSITIONS

1. on
2. beside
3. under
4. on top of
5. in front of
6. in
7. above
8. around
9. beneath

Page 4: LET'S COMPARE

1. Rita, Carol
2. Tom, George
3. House B, House A
4. Sparky, Jocko
5. Bob, Jim
6. Mary's car, Ken's car
7. B
8. C
9. A
10. A

Page 5: THE TELEPHONE

1. dial
2. receiver
3. cord
4. coin slot
5. coin return

Page 6: VERB FIT-IN

1. KEPT
2. RANG
3. LOST
4. SAT
5. MET
6. SENT
7. WON
8. SOLD
9. WORE
10. DROVE
11. ATE
12. FORGOT
13. BOUGHT
14. SWAM

Page 7: OPPOSITES

1. w, l
2. g, t
3. b, s
4. w, p
5. s, s
6. a, a
7. r, l
8. a, a
9. d, w
10. a, b
11. d, l
12. c, h
13. p, u
14. n, o
15. s, h

Page 8: TIME

1. two hours
2. one hour
3. one and one–half hours
4. four hours
5. thirty minutes
6. forty–five minutes
7. eight hours
8. six hours

66

Page 9: BUILD A WORD

1. ants, pants
2. ear, hear
3. ring, string
4. pins, spins
5. car, scar
6. river, driver
7. pills, spills
8. light, flight
9. rain, drain
10. hat, that

Page 10: RELATIONSHIPS

p
st
pa
cu
pl
su
au
te
ch
em
relationships

Page 11: WHERE ARE YOU?

at the airport

Page 12: WORD STAIRS

```
A C R O S S
        T
        U
        D
    Y E L L O W
            E
            E
        K N E E
            R
            A
            S
            E
        R O U N D
            O
            W
        N E X T
            A
            L
        L U N C H
            E
            L
            P
```

Page 13: ANIMALS

1. ant
2. frog
3. elephant
4. horse
5. rabbit
6. zebra
7. owl
8. deer
9. cow
10. bird
11. chicken
12. butterfly

Page 14: 2 + 2

one and nine-tenths —— 1.9
one–half —— 1/2
multiply —— ×
equal —— =
add —— +
one–third —— 1/3
sixty–eight hundredths —— .68
divide —— ÷
fiftieth —— 50th
percent —— %
subtract —— –
two–sevenths —— 2/7
zero —— 0
two–fourths —— 2/4
four – thousandths —— .004

Page 15: MONEY

PENNY
NICKEL
DIME
QUARTER
HALF DOLLAR
ONE DOLLAR BILL
FIVE DOLLAR BILL
TEN DOLLAR BILL
TWENTY DOLLAR BILL
FIFTY DOLLAR BILL
A PENNY SAVED IS A PENNY EARNED.

Page 16: THE BUS STATION

1. ATLANTA
2. BOSTON
3. DALLAS
4. DENVER
5. LAS VEGAS
6. MIAMI
7. NEW ORLEANS
8. NEW YORK
9. PITTSBURGH
10. PORTLAND
11. SAN ANTONIO
12. SAN FRANCISCO
THE BUS LEAVES ON TIME!

Page 17: CARS

hood   steering wheel   gas tank
windshield   roof   trunk   tail light
headlight   tire   door   door handle   bumper

Page 18: TWO-WORD VERBS

1. up
2. back
3. down
4. through
5. out
6. up
7. back
8. on
9. up
10. up
11. off
12. out
13. over
14. down
15. in
correct!

Page 19: AT THE RESTAURANT

Across:	Down:
1. tip	2. Coke
2. cold	3. dessert
4. coffee	4. cashier
6. steak	5. entree
11. menu	6. salad
12. cook	7. tea
13. salt	8. waiter
	10. lunch

Page 20: SIGNS

R_x —— drug store
Lead-free $1.27/gal. —— gas station
All Flights On Time —— airport
For Rent —— apartment
Next feature: 10 p.m. —— movie theater
Quiet Please! —— library
Speed Limit 55 mph —— highway
U.S. Mail —— post office
eggs 79¢/dozen —— supermarket
Don't Pick the Flowers —— park
Lot Filled —— parking lot
We have YOUR size! —— shoe store
Not For Hire —— taxi
Exact Change only —— bus
Open for Breakfast —— restaurant

Page 21: ADJECTIVES

One Syllable:	1. fifth
	2. cheap
Two Syllables:	1. secret
	2. absent
	3. busy
	4. correct
Three Syllables:	1. underlined
	2. registered
	3. personal
Four Syllables:	1. intelligent
	2. educated
	3. horizontal

Page 22: PAIRS

1. pepper	9. forth
2. down	10. uncle
3. wrong	11. short
4. out	12. bat
5. right	13. fork
6. dogs	14. day
7. sister	15. shut
8. leg	fine and dandy!

Page 23: ADVERBS

Answers will vary.

Page 24: SCHEDULES

R
I
G
H
T   RIGHT!

Page 25: CROSSWORD VERBS

Across: *Down:*
3. sleep   1. studied
5. understood   2. add
6. do   4. practices
7. washes   8. be
9. were   12. was
11. will go
13. left
14. walked
15. speaks

Page 26: BACKWARD/
FORWARD WORDS

1. twelve o'clock in the
   day —— noon
2. something you drink —— pop
3. another word for mother —— mom
4. a tiny child —— tot
5. past tense of do —— did
6. something a baby
   wears —— bib
7. another name for Robert —— Bob
8. a call for help —— SOS
9. an exclamation —— Wow!
10. energy —— pep
11. short for sister —— sis
12. another word for father —— dad

Page 27: THE MOVIES

1. Everyone likes to go to the
   movies.
2. People prefer different kinds of
   movies.
3. My father likes Westerns.
4. My mother likes mysteries.
5. My brother prefers science
   fiction.
6. My sister chooses love stories.
7. My best friend always wants to
   see monster movies.
8. My other friends go to
   comedies.
9. I go to everything.
10. I love the popcorn.

Page 28: TELEVISION

A T B T V S E T C D E F G
H E C I J O K L M N O P W
B L A C K A N D W H I T E
G E R N Q P R O G R A M A
A V T E M O V I E S R S T
M I O W S P O R T S T U H
E S O S V E W X Y Z A B E
S I N D E R F G C O L O R
H O S C H A N N E L I J K
A N T E N N A L M U H F N

Page 29: FAST FOOD AND
SNACKS

donuts, coffee, cereal
hot dogs, hamburgers
french fries, soup
pizza, fried chicken
T.V. dinner
candy
popcorn, soft drinks
potato chips, pretzels

Page 30: THE POST OFFICE

1. I went to the post office to mail a
   package.
2. I also wanted to buy some
   stamps.
3. The line was very long.
4. But it moved very quickly.
5. I sent the package first class.
6. The cost was $2.40.
7. I walked home slowly.
8. Then I remembered something.
9. I forgot to buy the stamps.
10. When I returned, the post office
    was closed.

Page 31: MUSIC! MUSIC!
MUSIC!

Answers will vary.

Page 32: AT THE BANK

1. Yesterday I went to the bank.
2. I stood in line for fifteen minutes.
3. I asked the teller to cash my check.
4. He gave me twenties and tens.
5. Then I went to speak to one of the officers.
6. She helped me open a savings account.
7. The officer gave me a free gift for opening the account.
8. I'll go again next week.

Page 33: COLORS

1. black, white
2. Yellow
3. green
4. brown
5. blue
6. orange
7. gray

IRREGULAR PLURALS

1. women
2. mice
3. children
4. men
5. teeth
6. feet

Page 34: DAYS AND MONTHS

Page 35: GROCERIES

cheese
milk
eggs
fish
chicken
carrots
bread
bananas
apples
cake
Lets eat!

Page 36: CONTRACTIONS

CAN'T
DON'T
ISN'T
DOESN'T
WE'RE
WHAT'S
COULDN'T
THEY'RE
I'M
YOU'RE
AREN'T
WHO'S
hidden word: CONTRACTIONS

Page 37: BODY PARTS

head	nose
eyes	ears
teeth	neck
arms	hands
legs	fingers
feet	knee

Page 38: FURNITURE

1. REFRIGERATOR
2. BATHTUB
3. RUG
4. PHONE
5. CHAIR
6. TABLE
7. COUCH
8. DRESSER
9. BED
hidden word: FURNITURE

Page 39: FAMILY

son, daughter
sister, brother
grandmother
husband
wife
aunt, uncle
aunt, uncle
cousins, sister
brother
father, grandfather

Page 40: HOME ACTIVITIES

is playing, is watching
is cooking, is washing
is cleaning, is brushing
is sleeping

Page 41: SEASONS AND WEATHER

Page 42: NUMBERS

Across:
1. two
4. fourteen
5. thirty three
9. eight
11. seventy
13. nine
14. fifteen

Down:
1. twenty seven
2. forty
3. one
6. fifty
7. sixty
8. eighty
10. twelve
12. ten

Page 43: CLOTHES

1. watch
2. tie
3. umbrella
4. dress
5. purse
6. hat
7. socks
8. fan
The closet is full.

Page 44: PAIRS

1. saucer
2. eggs
3. butter
4. chairs
5. socks
6. eggs
7. sugar
8. coat
9. cold
10. husband
11. comb
12. knife

OPPOSITES

floor
happy
present
in front of
easy
little
after
hello
a lot of
wrong
noon
dirty
day
closed
hidden message:
OPPOSITE WORDS

Page 45: VERBS WITH TIME EXPRESSIONS

1. answers
2. washed
3. accept
4. practices
5. will study
6. admits
7. comb
8. watched
9. will wear
10. carries
11. helped
12. agree
13. will celebrate
14. tries
15. invented
Everything is correct!

Page 46: SCHOOL

1. bus driver
2. English, teacher, assignments
3. soccer
4. mathematics, history, boring
5. science, homework, exercises
6. library
7. bookstore, notebooks, pencils, classmates, practice

Page 47: OCCUPATIONS

Across:
3. deliveryman
6. dietician
10. doctor
11. carpenter
12. painter
13. dentist
14. milkman
15. gardener

Down:
1. electrician
2. accountant
4. architect
5. photographer
7. farmer
8. salesman
9. reporter

Page 48: SIGNS

left column, top to bottom:
stop
railroad crossing
telephone
pedestrian crossing
school crossing
ladies' room
no animals

right column, top to bottom:
picnic area
yield
no smoking
handicapped
no left turn
men's room
poisonous
go

Page 49: FOLLOWING DIRECTIONS

drugstore
post office
bookstore
home
Right!

Page 50: PRODUCTS AND STORES

1.	I	7.	E
2.	H	8.	K
3.	G	9.	D
4.	A	10.	L
5.	B	11.	C
6.	J	12.	F

HOLIDAYS

1. money
2. animals
3. purple
4. gifts
5. June
6. office
7. red
8. vacation
9. snow

Page 51: SPORTS

clockwise from top left:
football
track
ice-skating
basketball
roller-skating
baseball
volleyball
ping pong
diving
fishing
skiing
badminton
racquetball
soccer
gymnastics
golf
hockey
boxing
tennis
swimming

Page 52: IRREGULAR
PAST TENSE

1. wrote
2. told
3. went
4. got
5. drank
6. gave
7. understood
8. had
9. came
10. ate
11. spoke
12. knew
13. saw
14. began
15. did

Page 53: TRANSPORTATION

Across:
1. truck
4. boat
7. bus
8. auto
10. drivers license
12. ship
13. car
14. ambulance
16. garage

Down:
1. taxi
2. chauffeur
3. motorcycle
5. train
6. horse
9. airplane
11. limousine
15. bike

Page 54: ENGLISH-SPEAKING
COUNTRIES

1. New Zealand
2. Ireland
3. Canada
4. Scotland
5. England
6. Australia
7. USA
8. India

TWO-WORD VERBS

1. out
2. down
3. on
4. down
5. off
6. through
7. down
8. over
9. over
10. for
11. back
hidden description: two word verb

Page 55: GOOD, BETTER, BEST

1. strongest
2. worst
3. cleanest
4. richest
5. best
6. thinner
7. younger
8. drier
9. more valuable

DON'T BELIEVE
EVERYTHING YOU HEAR

Page 56: DRUGSTORE

birthday card
calendar, comic books
magazines, newspapers
candy, ice cream
postcard, envelopes
record
alarm clock, cashier
sale, cheaply
aspirin

Page 57: TOOLS

Answers will vary.

Page 58: IRREGULAR PAST PARTICIPLES

1. bought/read, made, sung, stood, paid, bought
2. lost, found, worn
3. taken, fallen/been
4. flown/been, been, brought/ bought, said, shut, kept
5. forgotten, slept/been

Page 59: SOCIAL LIFE

Page 60: NEWSPAPER ADS

For Sale:
room, house
with, breakfast
and, family
fireplace
square, feet
garage, center
transportation

For Rent:
four, apartment
washer, carpet
living
bedroom
floor
basement
month

Wanted:
building
minutes
north
evenings

For Sale:
door
sedan
miles per gallon
air conditioning

You can find anything in the newspaper.

Page 61: EXPRESSIONS

1. dogs
2. low
3. stop
4. water
5. back
6. thin
7. out
8. down
9. left
10. take
11. short
12. go

FEELINGS

Answers will vary.

74

Page 62: JOB HUNTING

Across:
 1. check
 6. application
 9. employer
10. birth
12. sex
13. hire
14. days
15. weight

Down:
 2. employee
 3. interview
 4. job
 5. weekend
 7. part
 8. height
11. hours

Page 63: OTHER WAYS OF
SAYING THINGS I

 1. got out of
 2. call you up
 3. get better
 4. went back
 5. fill out
 6. looked through
 7. got in
 8. got sick

OTHER WAYS OF SAYING
THINGS II

 1. call me up
 2. write me
 3. very tired
 4. quit
 5. contact him
 6. Come over

Page 64: EMERGENCIES

help
dentist
broken, doctor, fire
department, police
accident, hospital
phone, book
operator, Neighbors